What Kind of Animal Is It?

Many Kinds of Animals

Molly Aloian and Bobbie Kalman

A Crabtree Crown Book

Crabtree Publishing
crabtreebooks.com

Many Kinds of Animals

Editor-in-chief
Bobbie Kalman

Writing team
Molly Aloian
Bobbie Kalman

Substantive editor
Kathryn Smithyman

Editors
Robin Johnson
Kelley MacAulay
Reagan Miller

Design
Margaret Salter

Consultant
Patricia Loesche, Ph.D.,
Animal Behavior Program,
Department of Psychology,
University of Washington

Production manager
Candice Campbell

Images
Shutterstock.com

Crabtree Publishing

crabtreebooks.com 800-387-7650

 In Canada: We acknowledge the financial support of the Government of Canada through the Canada Book Fund for our publishing activities.

Printed in the U.S.A./CP032026

Published in Canada
Crabtree Publishing
616 Welland Ave.
St. Catharines,
Ontario L2M 5V6

Published in the United States
Crabtree Publishing
347 Fifth Ave.
Suite 1402-145
New York, NY 10016

Hardcover: 978-1-0398-7320-9
Paperback: 978-1-0398-7378-0
Ebook (pdf): 978-1-0398-7427-5
Epub: 978-1-0398-7476-3

Library and Archives Canada Cataloguing in Publication
Available at Library and Archives Canada

Library of Congress Cataloging-in-Publication Data
Available at the Library of Congress

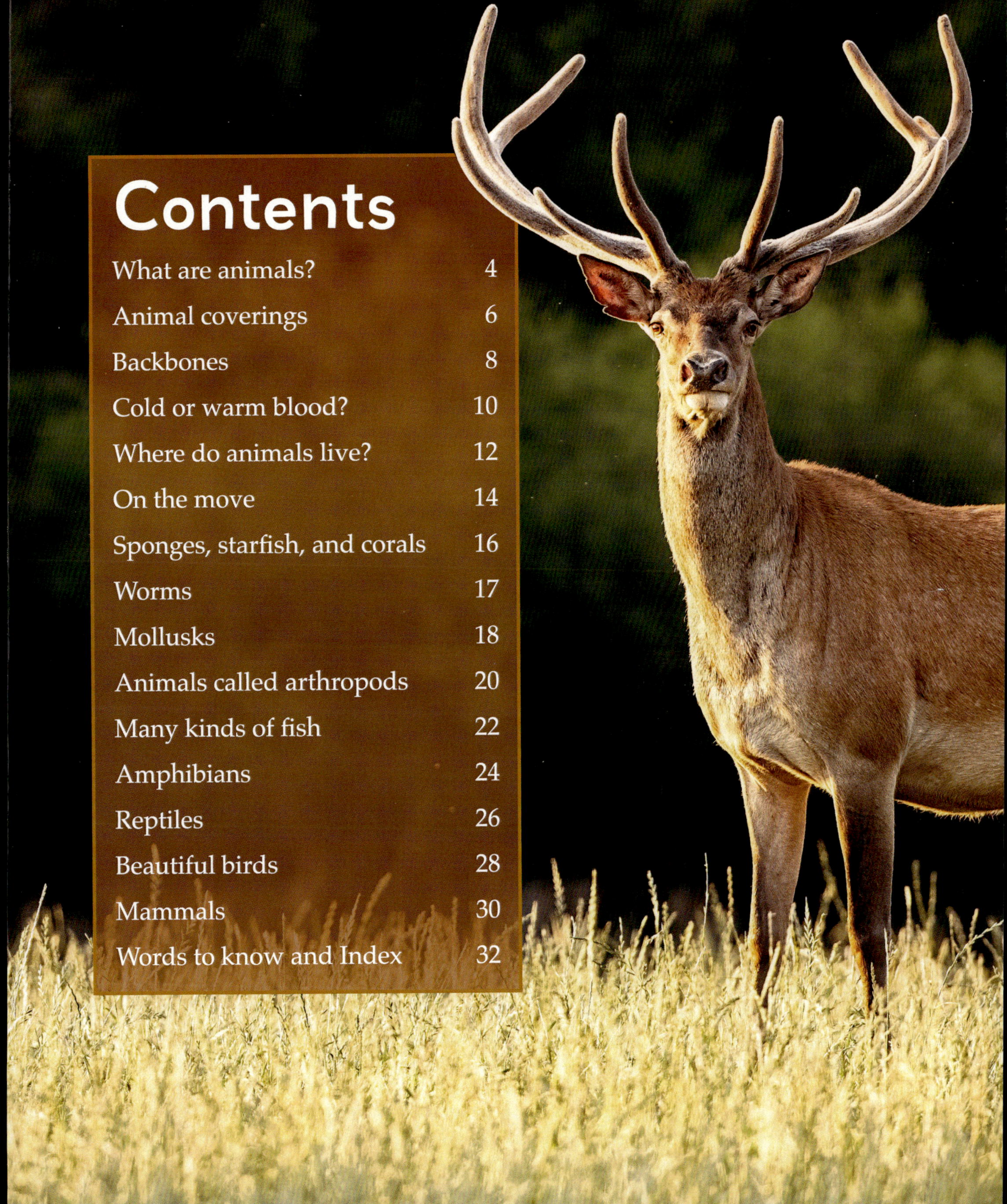

Contents

What are animals?

Animals are living things. They are found all over the world. Some animals live in water, and others live on land. There are many groups of animals. Some of the groups are shown on these pages. How many of these animals do you know?

fish

Fish

Fish are one group of animals.

snail

Mollusks

Snails belong to a group of animals called **mollusks**.

Worms

Worms make up a group of animals. There are many kinds of worms.

worm

Amphibians

Amphibians are another group of animals. Frogs are amphibians.

frog

spider

Arthropods

Arthropods are a group of animals that includes spiders.

Reptiles

Snakes belong to a group of animals called **reptiles**.

snake

Birds

Birds make up their own group of animals.

bird

Mammals

One group of animals is called **mammals**. Bears and cats are mammals. People are mammals, too.

cat

bear

Animal coverings

Different animals have different coverings on their bodies. Mammals have fur or hair. Reptiles are covered in **scales**. Birds are covered in feathers. Arthropods are covered in **exoskeletons**.

A snake is a reptile. Snakes have scales on their bodies.

A beetle is an arthropod. Beetles have exoskeletons. Exoskeletons are hard cases.

Most fish are also covered in scales.

A snail is a mollusk. Snails have hard shells covering their bodies.

Birds have feathers on their bodies. Feathers help birds fly.

People are mammals. People have hair.

This dog is a mammal. Dogs are covered in fur.

A salamander is an amphibian. Salamanders have smooth, slimy skin.

Backbones

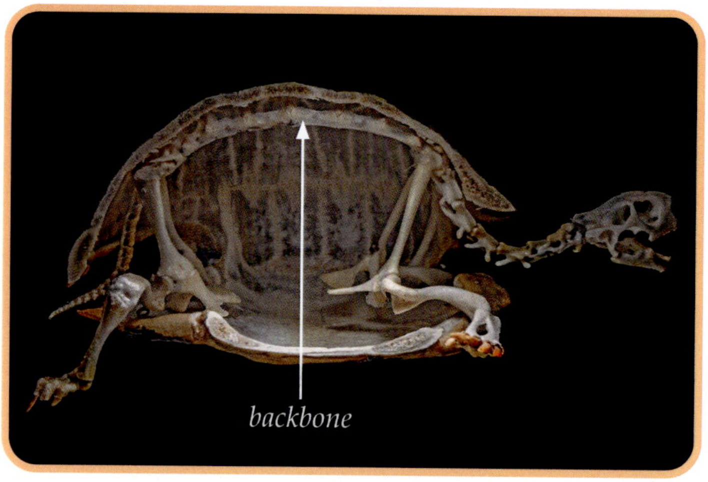

Some animals have **backbones** inside their bodies. A backbone is a group of bones in the middle of an animal's back. People have backbones, too!

A tortoise's backbone is inside its body.

The tortoise's shell is attached to its backbone.

No backbones

Most of the animals on Earth do not have backbones. In fact, they do not have any bones at all!

Jellyfish do not have backbones.

Millipedes do not have backbones.

Slugs do not have backbones.

Soft bodies

Many animals without backbones have soft bodies. Octopuses have soft bodies. An octopus is a mollusk.

Cold or warm blood?

Most animals are **cold-blooded**. The body temperature of a cold-blooded animal does not stay the same. It changes. When the weather is warm, the animal's body is warm. When the weather is cold, the animal's body is cold. If a cold-blooded animal needs to warm up, it sits in the sun.

Reptiles are cold-blooded animals.

This bullfrog is a cold-blooded amphibian. It is sitting in the sun to warm its body.

Warm blood

Warm-blooded animals have warm bodies. Their body temperatures do not change much. They stay about the same, even when the animals are in cold places. Mammals such as bears are warm-blooded animals. People are also warm-blooded.

Birds are warm-blooded animals. A parrot is a kind of bird.

Where do animals live?

Different animals live in different **habitats**. A habitat is the natural place where an animal lives. Forests, deserts, and fields are animal habitats. Some animals even live in freezing cold places!

Cold and icy

The penguins shown below are birds. They live in Antarctica. Antarctica is a place that is always cold. Most of Antarctica is covered with snow and ice. Penguins live on the ice and swim in the cold water.

Many lizards live in hot deserts. Deserts are habitats that get very little rain.

Raccoons live in forests. This raccoon's home is in a tree.

Living in water

Fish and many other kinds of animals live in water. Most of the animals that live in water can swim. Some animals that live on land are also able to swim. Name three land animals that can swim. Are you a swimmer?

Sea otters live in water.

On the move

Animals move from place to place in different ways. Some animals walk or run. Some jump. Some animals fly, and some swim. Look at how these animals are moving. How do you move in water? How do you move up a hill?

A butterfly flies by flapping its wings.

Horses walk or run. They can also swim and jump.

Most birds can fly. This osprey flies from place to place looking for food.

On land, a tiger walks or runs. In water, a tiger swims.

A snake ***slithers****. To slither means to slide on the belly.*

A kangaroo jumps. It has strong back legs for jumping.

A grasshopper is another animal that jumps.

Sponges, starfish, and corals

Sponges, starfish, and corals do not look like animals, but they are animals! These animals do not have heads or brains. Sponges, starfish, and corals live in oceans.

A starfish has a simple body. It has five arms that all look the same.

This tube sponge looks like a plant, but it is an animal.

Corals come in different colors. They can be pink, orange, or green.

Worms

There are many kinds of worms. Some worms live under the ground. Other worms live in oceans. Worms that live under the ground have soft, long, thin bodies. Some of the worms that live in oceans look like Christmas trees!

Christmas tree worms live in oceans.

Earthworms live in the ground. This earthworm is in a ***burrow****. A burrow is an underground home.*

Bristle worms live in oceans, too. They have tiny hairs called ***bristles*** *on their bodies.*

Mollusks

Mollusks are animals with soft bodies. They do not have backbones. Most mollusks have shells. Some mollusks live on land. Other mollusks live in water. The flame scallop, shown below, is a mollusk that lives in water.

A clam has two shells that protect its soft body.

A snail is a mollusk with a shell.

Squids

A squid is a mollusk that does not have a shell. A squid has one eye on each side of its head. It also has eight arms on its head.

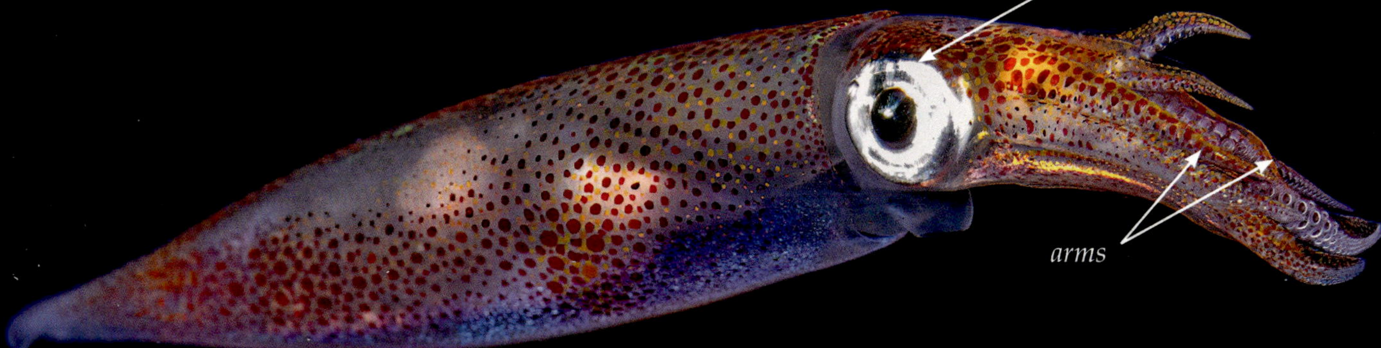

Animals called arthropods

A spider has eight legs. Each of its legs can bend.

There are millions of arthropods on Earth. All arthropods have legs that bend. Insects, crabs, and spiders are arthropods.

A lot of legs!

Insects are arthropods with six legs. Spiders are arthropods with eight legs. There are even arthropods with more than one hundred legs!

A crab is an arthropod that has ten legs.

Some kinds of millipedes have more than one hundred legs!

Wonderful wings

Some arthropods have wings. Butterflies, bees, and flies are arthropods that have wings. These arthropods use their wings to fly from place to place.

Many butterflies have colorful wings.

Many kinds of fish

Fish live in water. They are cold-blooded animals with backbones. Most fish have scales all over their bodies. Fish come in many shapes, colors, and sizes. Some fish are very small. Other fish are big. Some sharks are huge!

A sea horse may not look like a fish, but it is a fish!

A moray eel is a fish that looks like a snake!

Fish fins

Fish do not have legs for moving from place to place. Instead, they have **fins**. Fish use their fins to swim through water. Fins come in different shapes and sizes.

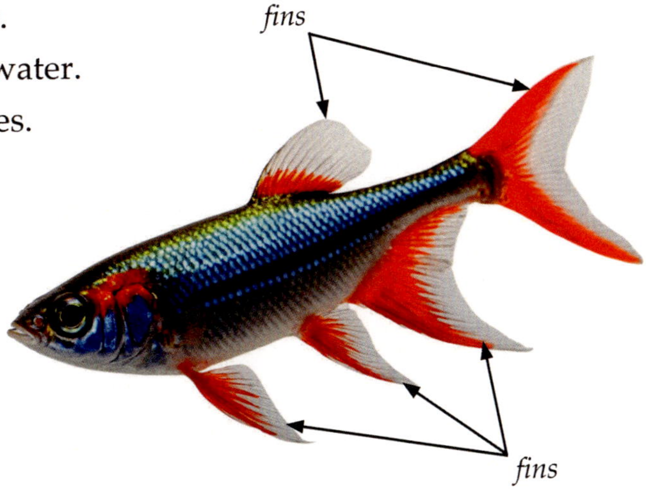

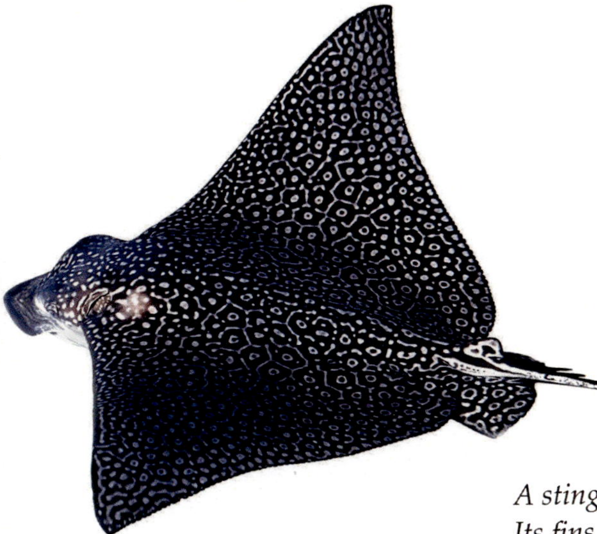

A stingray is a kind of fish. Its fins are shaped like wings.

This shark has big fins. Sharks use their big fins to swim quickly.

Amphibians

A baby frog is called a ***tadpole****. A tadpole lives in water. An adult frog lives on land.*

Frogs and toads are amphibians. Amphibians are animals that live in water and on land. When they are babies, amphibians live in water. When they are adults, amphibians live on land.

Toads and frogs

It is often hard to see the difference between a toad and a frog. A toad usually has bumpy, dry skin. A frog usually has smooth, wet skin. A toad has short back legs. A frog's back legs are longer.

The skin of this toad is covered with bumps.

Amphibians with tails

Salamanders and newts are amphibians. These animals have tails. Frogs and toads do not have tails.

salamander

newt

Some snakes are very long.

Reptiles

Turtles and lizards are two kinds of reptiles. Most reptiles have four legs, but some do not have any legs!

How big?

Some reptiles are small. A gecko is a small reptile. Other reptiles are big. Crocodiles and alligators are big, strong reptiles.

A lizard is a reptile. Like all reptiles, lizards are covered with scales.

A sea turtle lives in water most of the time.

Shells

Turtles and tortoises are reptiles. Turtles live mainly in water. Tortoises live on land. Both turtles and tortoises have shells. These animals move slowly on land because their shells are heavy.

A tortoise has strong legs to help it carry its heavy shell.

Beautiful birds

These parrots have colorful feathers.

There are many kinds of birds on Earth. Some birds are big, and others are tiny. Birds are the only animals that are covered in feathers. Birds have two wings. Most birds can fly, but a few kinds of birds cannot fly.

An ostrich has wings, but it cannot fly. It runs on its long, strong legs.

What a beak!

All birds have beaks. Beaks can be long and narrow or short and curved. Many birds use their beaks to build homes called **nests**. Birds also find food with their beaks. They then use their beaks to carry the food they find.

The crane is a bird that lives in water. It uses its long beak to catch fish.

Baby birds are called ***chicks****. These chicks have their beaks wide open. They are in their nest, waiting to be fed.*

The toucan uses its big beak to pick fruit from trees. It also uses its beak to catch insects and small reptiles to eat.

Mammals

Mammals are warm-blooded animals. All mammals have backbones. There are many kinds of mammals. Cats, dogs, horses, whales, and dolphins are mammals. People are mammals, too!

This boy and his cat are both mammals. You are also a mammal!

Some mammals live in water. Dolphins are mammals that live in water.

Mammal babies

Most mammal mothers take care of their babies. Mother mammals make milk inside their bodies to feed to their babies. Mammal babies drink milk for weeks or months. When the babies are old enough, their mothers teach them how to find food on their own.

Baby mammals look like their parents.

Baby mammals ***nurse****, or drink milk from the bodies of their mothers. These four kittens are nursing.*

Words to know and Index

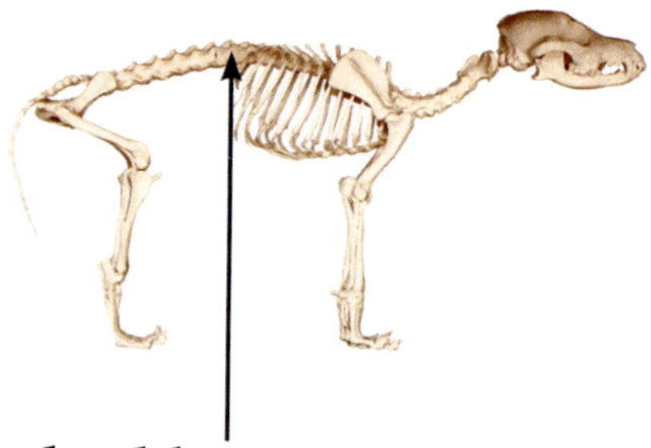

desert

forest